Phonics

This book belongs to

Alphabet Critter

Say the alphabet. Write the missing letters.

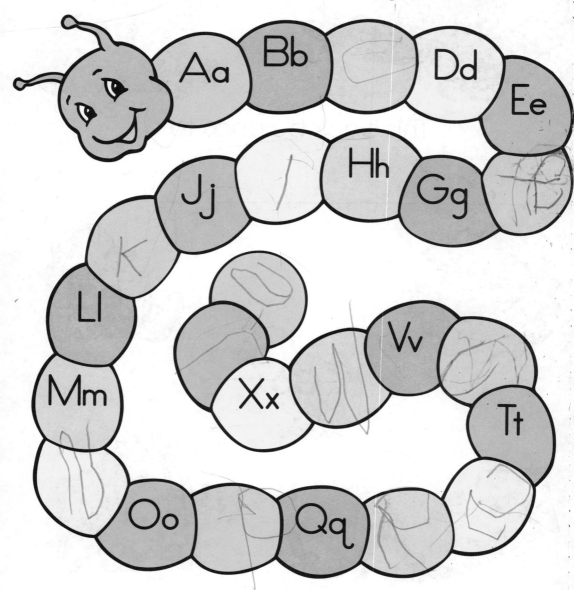

2

Follow the Path

Say the alphabet. Write the missing letters.

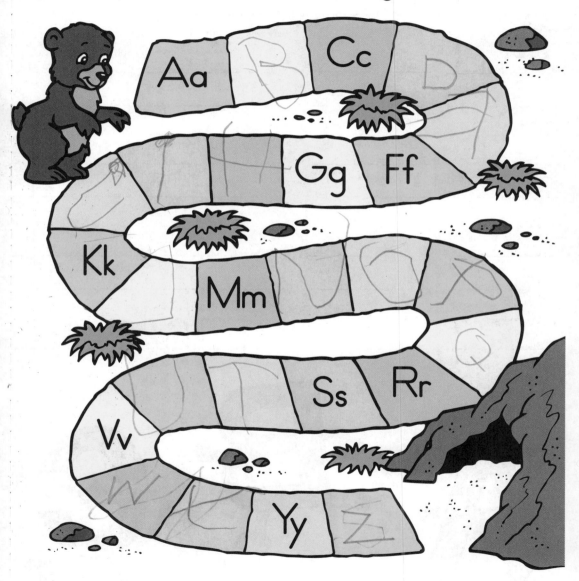

FS109026 • Phonics

Trace and Write

Trace the letters. Write each letter.

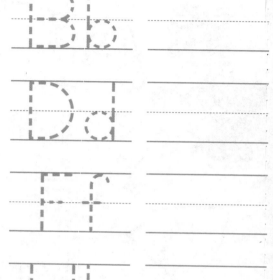

Trace and Write

Trace the letters. Write each letter.

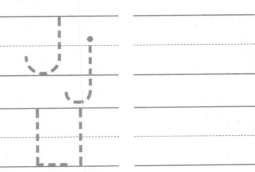

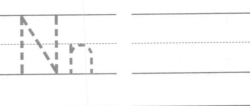

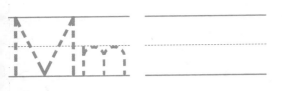

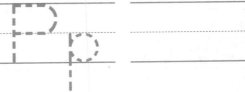

5

Trace and Write

Trace the letters. Write each letter.

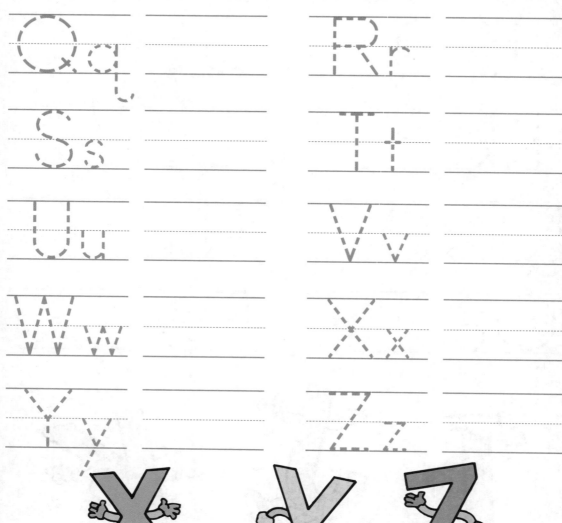

© Carson-Dellosa

FS109026 • Phonics

Off to School

Connect the dots from **A** to **Z**.

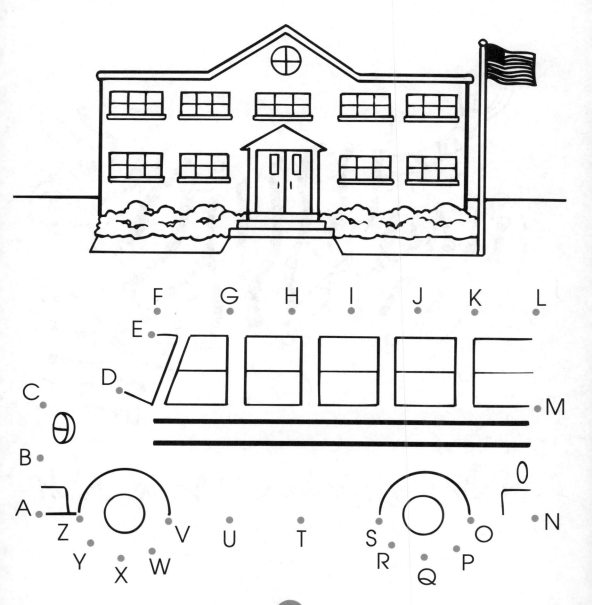

© Carson-Dellosa

FS109026 • Phonics

A Zoo Animal

Connect the dots from **a** to **z**.

Letter Matchup

In each row, circle the letters that match the first letter.

B B B R P

C Q O C C

D D P D O

F P F E F

© Carson-Dellosa   FS109026 • Phonics

More Matching

In each row, circle the letters that match the first letter.

b	p	b	q	b
c	c	q	o	c
d	p	d	o	d
f	p	f	t	f

Little Critters

Draw lines to match the capital letters on the caterpillars to the lowercase letters on the butterflies.

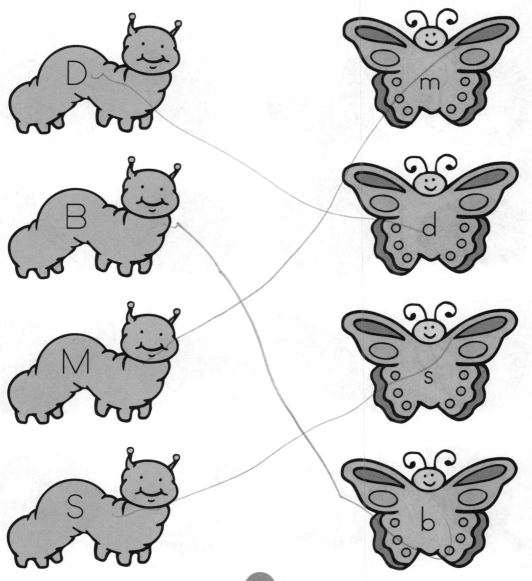

Beginning Sounds

Look at the first picture in each row. Say its name. Circle the pictures that have the same beginning sound.

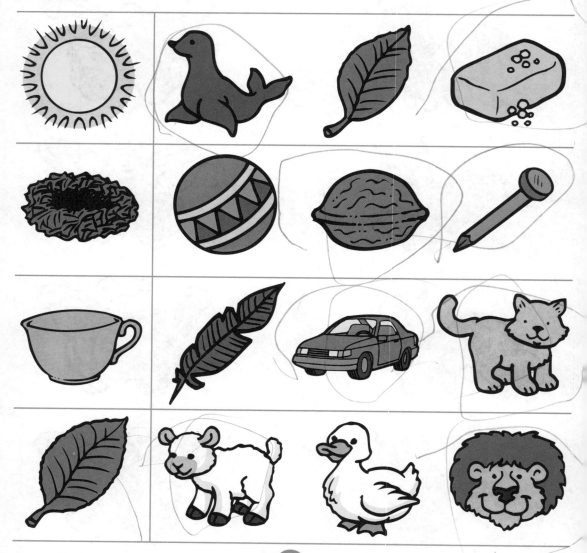

Food Fun

Look at the first picture in each row. Say its name. Color the picture that has the same beginning sound.

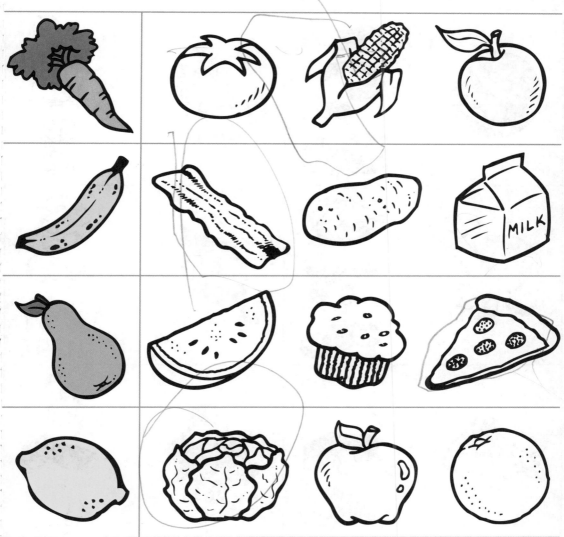

Same Sounds

Look at each box. Say the name of the picture on the left. Draw lines from it to the pictures that have the same beginning sound.

FS109026 • Phonics

Rhyme Time

Look at the pictures in each pair. Say their names.
Draw a line to match the pictures if they rhyme.

FS109026 • Phonics

Fun with Rhymes

Name the first picture in each row. Color the pictures that rhyme with it.

The Sound of B

Look at the pictures. Say their names.
Listen for the **b** sound at the beginning
of each word. Trace the letters
and color the pictures.

Bb

ball

bed

banana

bear

balloon

B B B B B B B

b b b b b b b b

17

The Sound of C

Look at the pictures. Say their names. Listen for the c sound at the beginning of each word. Trace the letters and color the pictures.

car

corn

cat

carrot

camel

FS109026 • Phonics

The Sound of D

Look at the pictures. Say their names. Listen for the **d** sound at the beginning of each word. Trace the letters and color the pictures.

Dd

dog

door

doll

duck

D D D D D D D

d d d d d d d

Letters and Sounds

Trace the letters. Circle the pictures that have the same beginning sound as each letter.

The Sound of F

Look at the pictures. Say their names. Listen for the **f** sound at the beginning of each word. Trace the letters and color the pictures.

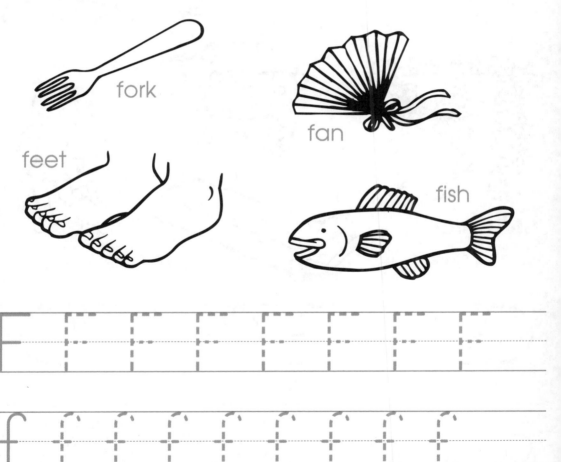

fork

fan

feet

fish

© Carson-Dellosa

The Sound of G

Look at the pictures. Say their names. Listen for the **g** sound at the beginning of each word. Trace the letters and color the pictures.

goat

garden

gum

girl

The Sound of H

Look at the pictures. Say their names. Listen for the **h** sound at the beginning of each word. Trace the letters and color the pictures.

hat

hand

horse

house

Listen Carefully

Look at each column. Color the pictures that begin with the letter shown at the top.

Ff	Gg	Hh

The Sound of J

Look at the pictures. Say their names. Listen for the j sound at the beginning of each word. Trace the letters and color the pictures.

Jj

jeans

jar

jump rope

jeep

FS109026 • Phonics

The Sound of K

Look at the pictures. Say their names. Listen for the **k** sound at the beginning of each word. Trace the letters and color the pictures.

Kk

key

kangaroo

kite

king

The Sound of L

Look at the pictures. Say their names. Listen for the **l** sound at the beginning of each word. Trace the letters and color the pictures.

leaf

lemon

lamp

ladder

FS109026 • Phonics

Listen to the Letter Sounds

Trace the letters on each object. Circle the pictures whose names begin with the letters.

The Sound of M

Look at the pictures. Say their names. Listen for the **m** sound at the beginning of each word. Trace the letters and color the pictures.

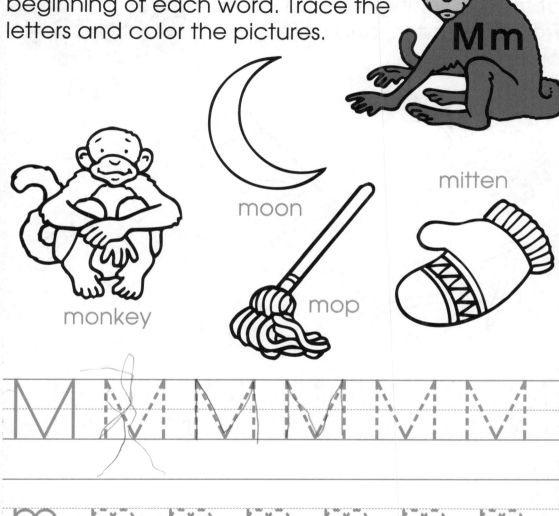

Mm

moon

mitten

monkey

mop

© Carson-Dellosa

FS109026 • Phonics

The Sound of N

Look at the pictures. Say their names. Listen for the **n** sound at the beginning of each word. Trace the letters and color the pictures.

Nn

nest

napkin

nails

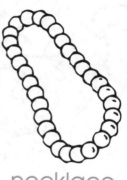

necklace

N N N N N N N

n n n n n n n

The Sound of P

Look at the pictures. Say their names. Listen for the **p** sound at the beginning of each word. Trace the letters and color the pictures.

Pp

pizza

pig

pool

pumpkin

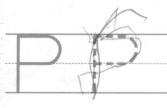

Pictures and Sounds

Draw lines from the letters to the pictures that have the same beginning sound.

The Sound of Q

Look at the pictures. Say their names. Listen for the **q** sound at the beginning of each word. Trace the letters and color the pictures.

quarter

question

queen

quilt

The Sound of R

Look at the pictures. Say their names. Listen for the **r** sound at the beginning of each word. Trace the letters and color the pictures.

ring

rainbow

rabbit

radio

R R R R R R R

r r r r r r r

The Sound of S

Look at the pictures. Say their names. Listen for the **s** sound at the beginning of each word. Trace the letters and color the pictures.

Ss

sun

soap

sock

sandwich

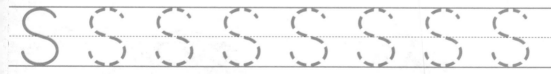

S S S S S S S S S

S S S S S S S S S

Super Sounds

Circle the pair of letters in each box that make the same beginning sound as the picture.

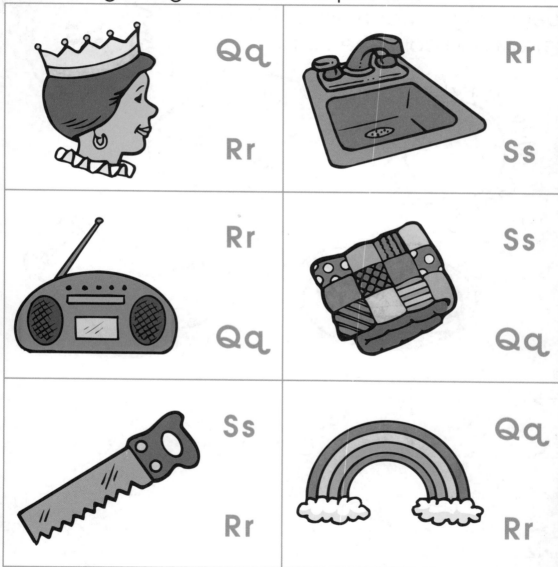

Qq

Rr

Rr

Ss

Rr

Qq

Ss

Qq

Ss

Rr

Qq

Rr

36

The Sound of T

Look at the pictures. Say their names. Listen for the **t** sound at the beginning of each word. Trace the letters and color the pictures.

toaster

towel

toothbrush

telephone

The Sound of V

Look at the pictures. Say their names. Listen for the **v** sound at the beginning of each word. Trace the letters and color the pictures.

volcano

vegetables

van

vase

The Sound of W

Look at the pictures. Say their names. Listen for the **w** sound at the beginning of each word. Trace the letters and color the pictures.

worm

window

wagon

waterfall

W W W W W W W W W

W W W W W W W W W

Matching Sounds

Draw lines from each letter to the pictures with the same beginning sound.

Tt

Vv

 Ww

Ww

Vv

Tt

40

The Sound of X

Look at the pictures. Say their names. Listen for the **x** sound at the end of each word. Trace the letters and color the pictures.

Xx

six

box

fox

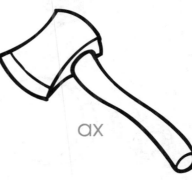

ax

X ✕ ✕ ✕ ✕ ✕ ✕ ✕

X ✕ ✕ ✕ ✕ ✕ ✕ ✕

FS109026 • Phonics

The Sound of Y

Look at the pictures. Say their names. Listen for the **y** sound at the beginning of each word. Trace the letters and color the pictures.

yarn

yo-yo

yawn

yellow

Y Y Y Y Y Y Y

y y y y y y y

42

The Sound of Z

Look at the pictures. Say their names. Listen for the **z** sound at the beginning of each word. Trace the letters and color the pictures.

Zz

zoo

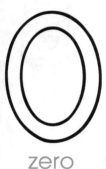

zero

zebra

zipper

Z Z Z Z Z Z Z

Z Z Z Z Z Z Z

FS109026 • Phonics

Can You Hear the Sounds?

Circle the pictures that have the same beginning or ending sound as the letters.

Begins with **Y y**

Begins with **Z z**

Ends with **X x**

FS109026 • Phonics

Listen and Trace

Listen for the beginning sound of each picture.
Trace the letter that makes the beginning sound.

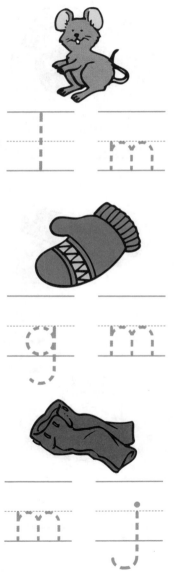

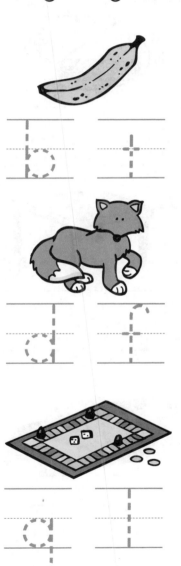

FS109026 • Phonics

Listen and Trace

Listen for the beginning sound of each picture.
Trace the letter that makes the beginning sound.

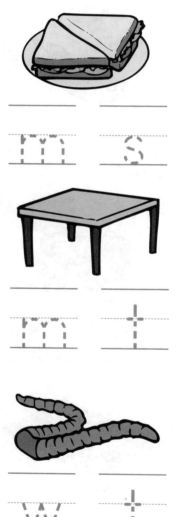

m   s

i   c

m   t

n   g

w   t

c   s

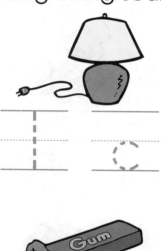

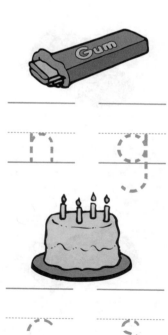

FS109026 • Phonics

Letter Sounds

Trace the letters. Color the pictures that begin with each letter.

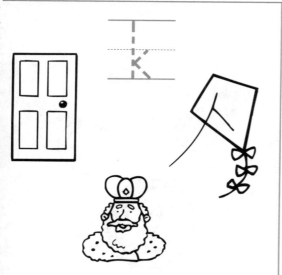

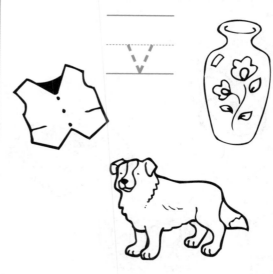

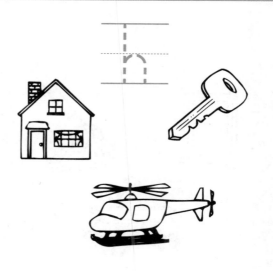

FS109026 • Phonics

Trace and Color

Trace the letters. Color the pictures that begin with each letter.

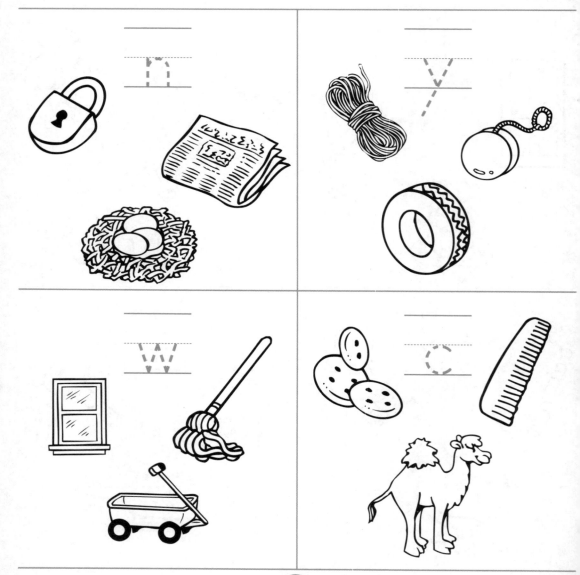

FS109026 • Phonics

Letter Challenge

Trace the letters. Color the pictures that begin with each letter.

FS109026 • Phonics

Listen and Write

Look at each picture. Say its name. Write the letter it begins with in the box beneath.

Vowel Sounds

Look at the pictures in the clouds. Say the vowel sounds. Trace the letters and color the pictures.

FS109026 • Phonics

Sky-High Vowels

Say the names of the pictures. Listen to the vowel sounds. Write the matching lowercase vowel on each kite.

© Carson-Dellosa

FS109026 • Phonics

Ending Sounds

Listen for the ending sound of each picture. Write it at the end of each word.

ba

bu

cu

he

mu

More Ending Sounds

Listen for the ending sound of each picture. Write it at the end of each word.

tu_____

fa_____

to_____

be_____

ca_____

pi_____

Beginning and End

Say the names of the pictures. Write the letters that make the beginning and ending sounds.

_____

a

_____

o

_____

a

_____

o

_____

e

_____

u

knows letters and sounds!

Great job!

_____
signature

_____
date

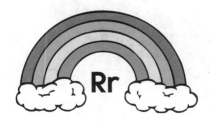

FS109026 • Phonic